POINTS OF VIEW

George Pifer
Nancy Whisler Mutoh

Japanese-American Conversation Institute
Tokyo, Japan

NEWBURY HOUSE PUBLISHERS, INC. / ROWLEY / MASSACHUSETTS

Library of Congress Cataloging in Publication Data

Pifer, George.
  Points of view.

  1. English language--Text-books for foreigners.
I. Mutoh, Nancy, joint author. II. Title.
PE1128.P5   428.2'4'07   77-972
ISBN 0-88377-072-5

Cover design by June Durante.

NEWBURY HOUSE PUBLISHERS, Inc.

Language Science
Language Teaching
Language Learning

Rowley, Massachusetts 01969

Printed in the U.S.A.   First printing: April 1977
                                        10   9   8   7

To the Teacher

ANALYSIS and PROBLEM SOLVING

The two types of case studies in this book, *Analysis* and *Problem Solving,* have different purposes, and, therefore, the way you handle them in class should reflect this.

The purpose of the *Analysis* section is to give the students practice in reading carefully and analytically. After reading each story, the students must rank the relative importance of certain ideas related to the actions of the characters in the stories. Some of the ideas are clearly brought out in the story, and the students should be encouraged to point to specific sentences that support their ranking of these items. Other items are not mentioned directly, but by reading the story carefully and getting a "feel" for the characters, students should be able to rank some of the items by inference and, again, should be encouraged to point out sentences that support their ranking. Sometimes a certain item isn't mentioned in the story at all. In this case, it also requires a good reader to recognize this. In these cases, the item should just be left blank. Therefore, reading carefully and being able to justify one's analysis of a reading selection are the main skills emphasized in this first type of case study. After the analysis work, the students also have a chance to discuss their own personal opinions about the subject of the story, but these opinions should be kept separate from and not projected into the analysis activities.

The second type of case study, *Problem Solving*, in addition to analysis, also emphasizes different elements of group discussion such as brain-storming, critically evaluating different proposed courses of action, presenting individual opinions and arguing in their favor, and working toward a group concensus. In these case studies, a situation is described in general terms, but not all of the details are specified. The purpose of the "openness" is to give the students a chance to project themselves and their own culture into the situation and fill in the details in a way that seems most realistic to them. Since all the case studies are based on everyday problems and situations, they give the students a chance to discuss their feelings about real life situations we all face and, therefore, to interact with the language and with each other on a more personal level than most material provides.

GENERAL PROCEDURES

Both types of case studies are based on small group discussions (about four to six students per group), alternating with individual work. Depending on your own students, the amount of class time available, etc., you can assign the individual work to be done either at home or in class. After the small group discussions, you might also want to have a full class discussion based on summarized reports from each small group. In both types of studies, each step is accompanied by brief directions to the students, but, before beginning the first case study of each type, you might want to go through the instructions once with the whole class to be sure the students understand the overall procedure.

During the small group discussions, you should go around to each group and listen. The students should carry the initiative, even if it means struggling sometimes with moments of silence or with the frustration of searching for a way to express an idea. After students become accustomed to working in small groups, they will all pitch in to help each other. One of your most important functions is to set an example for the listeners by occasionally asking a student to point out the sentences in the story that support his ranking of a certain item or to explain the specific advantages and disadvantages he or she sees in one course of action over another. By following your example, the students should become more careful and critical listeners, forcing the speaker also to try to be as clear and persuasive as possible.

TAILORING THE CASE STUDIES TO YOUR STUDENTS

Since the kinds of students studying English as a foreign or second language vary tremendously, we have tried to choose subjects for these case studies which are as universal as possible, make them sufficiently open to allow students to project themselves into the situations, and then provide a variety of supplementary exercises and material.

In the classroom it is up to you to use the material in a way that is appropriate for the age, level of proficiency, and socio-economic background of your students. For better students, the individual work can all be done at home, and class time devoted exclusively to discussion. For other students, it might be helpful to have a session of comprehension questions and answers on the story before moving into small group discussions. Also, the case studies are written from a variety of points of view—middle-aged and young, male and female, parent and child, etc. You should encourage each student to consider the situation from his or her own point of view in the steps calling for personal opinions. As you choose which supplementary exercises to assign, you will find some that are more relevant to your particular students than others, so this decision should also be a considered one.

To the Student

You have already studied quite a lot of English grammar, have learned a basic vocabulary, and have done quite a bit of reading. The purpose of this book is to give you practice in speaking English.

This book consists of case studies which describe situations and problems that we all face in everyday life. You will read about a situation and think about it. Then you will work with other students in a small group to analyze that situation. You should follow the directions given for each step.

The purposes of these activities are: (1) to work with other students to improve everyone's fluency in expressing ideas; (2) to use English as a *means of* communication, but not as the purpose or end of communication—in other words active English; (3) to help you begin thinking in English, since not only the reading and discussion, but also the analysis has to be done in English; (4) to learn some vocabulary and expressions that are useful in talking about everyday situations and problems; (5) to give you a chance to express your own ideas about these situations and problems.

SPECIFIC PROCEDURES

Problem Solving Case Studies

STEP ONE

Individual: Each student reads the story, putting him- or herself into the situation and imagining his or her own feelings and reactions if faced with the problem.

STEP TWO

Group: The students try to brainstorm as many possible courses of action as they can. They don't evaluate or criticize any of the ideas—only try to write down as many as possible.

STEP THREE

Group: The students proceed to discuss the advantages and disadvantages of their ideas from Step Two. Each person makes his or her own decision about which courses of action he or :

Analysis Case Studies

Individual: Each student reads the story, trying to understand each character's way of thinking and feeling and trying not to project his or her own ideas into the story.

Individual: Based on his or her analysis, each student looks at the ideas listed and tries to rank their relative importance from the point of view of the characters in the story, *not* from his or her own point of view.

Group: Students tell each other their rankings from Step Two and explain, by pointing to specific sentences in the story, how they made their ranking decisions.

Step Three (continued): she thinks are best and worst and explains his or her reasoning to the group. If possible, they can try to come to a group concensus.

Individual: Each student now can consider his or her own opinions about the ideas in Step Two. Each student should rank the items according to his or her own feelings about the situation.

STEP FOUR

Individual: Each student considers his or her own personal opinions about the general issues involved in the situation by completing the statements in this step.

Group: Students compare and discuss their opinions recorded in Step Four. This discussion should also include reasons and examples to clarify and illustrate the opinions each student has.

STEP FIVE

Group: Students compare and discuss their opinions recorded in Step Four. This discussion should include reasons and examples to clarify and illustrate the opinion each student has.

Preface

CASE STUDIES

In applying the case study approach to second and foreign language learning, we feel the following three characteristics of these case studies contribute to best results. First, the subject matter of each study poses a situation or problem taken from daily life. Second, each study presents the participants with a series of tasks that give their thinking and discussion direction. The goal is not merely to understand the information in a particular study, but to use it in order to make value judgments, analyze people's behavior, or evaluate alternate courses of action. Third, the situations in each study are not specified in complete detail. This gives the participants the chance to project their own cultural and individual ideas into each situation, making it more applicable to themselves personally.

LANGUAGE LEARNING THROUGH CASE STUDIES

We believe that language learning means learning to com-municate. Communication requires a social context as well as trial and error attempts to understand and be understood. In addition to providing the "occasion to communicate," we feel these case studies also provide the occasion to learn and practice the following language components and skills:

1. **Vocabulary and syntax in context.** The studies introduce vocabulary and structures that naturally occur while talking about daily life situations or decisions. Students learn these words and structures in a meaningful context and then have to use them immediately in the various tasks required by each study. Since each task builds on the previous one, there is a natural check on whether students correctly understand the meaning carried in the vocabulary and syntax.

2. **Reading comprehension.** Each situation is presented as a reading. Students must read correctly in order to use the information as raw material for the tasks of analysis or decision-making. Students must support their analyses in their discussion groups by pointing to relevant sentences in the readings.

3. **Listening comprehension and self-expression.** When students become interested in the situations presented, their desire to communicate increases. They become more attentive listeners who ask for clarification or repetition when they lose the speaker's train of thought. They also have to correct any gross pronunciation or syntactic errors which prevent them from getting their ideas across. While discussing, students have a chance to develop such useful skills as paraphrasing, simplifying, summarizing, exemplifying, and elaborating, and these lead to greater confidence as communicators.

4. **Discussion and argumentation.** The tasks require making judgments concerning the situations, and discussing these judgments in small groups. Each participant wants the others in his group to, if not agree with him, then at least understand his decision or judgment and consider it reasonable. This provides practice in the skills of organizing thoughts, marshaling supportive details from the readings, and persuasively answering questions or challenges from other group members.

5. **Writing.** Some of the tasks require students to make a list of the advantages and disadvantages of given alternatives or to make their own list of possible courses of action. Students can also be asked to write follow-up essays explaining their individual decisions.

6. **Problem-solving.** Since the activities in these case studies all represent certain steps or procedures in an empirical approach to problem-solving, they give the students exposure to and practice in that way of analyzing and handling real situations.

7. **Reflecting on individual and cultural values.** All decisions in these case studies, as in real life, are based on people's frame of values. These activities cause students consciously to consider their own values. In bi- or multi-cultural groups, this presents an excellent occasion for cross-cultural learning. Because many vocabulary items are culturally "loaded," both in real life and these case studies, developing sensitivity to the range of meaning and depth of individual words helps students become better communicators.

ADVANTAGES OF CASE STUDIES

1. **Thinking in English.** Because the emphasis is not on the language itself, but rather on using the language as a medium to accomplish an interesting activity, there is less tendency for students to insist on translating everything back into their own

language. Also the nature of the tasks requires students to analyze (therefore think) in English since they have to (a) understand the individual sentences in the stories, (b) understand the interrelationship of the sentences as they qualify or support each other, (c) reach an understanding of the overall situation, and (d) use that understanding of the whole as well as the parts as a tool in analyzing and decision-making.

2. **Motivation.** Because students perceive the situations as real life matters, they are drawn into wanting to talk about them. In order to do that, they need certain vocabulary and syntactical items. It is generally recognized that people who want to learn succeed in learning and retaining the material the best.

3. **Class rapport.** Discussing matters of personal interest in small rotating groups gives students a real chance to get to know each other as people. Only when this happens can the language classroom become a place where people want to communicate. And only if people want to communicate can they be efficient and motivated language learners.

4. **Stimulation of small group discussion.** When placed in a small group, given a topic, and told by the teacher to "discuss," many students have a hard time developing an interesting conversation. Case studies overcome this problem by providing direction and purpose in the form of tasks. Therefore, even in a large class, by breaking into case study groups, every student has the chance to do a lot of worthwhile talking and interacting in English.

5. **Material for intermediate and advanced students.** After learning a certain amount of grammar and vocabulary in the early stages of language study, students want to and need to have a chance to use their knowledge. There is a lack of material of this type which allows students to try out their ability within a situation structured enough to give them help and direction. Case studies have proven to be one effective way to meet this need.

Contents

I Analysis

Getting Married

Photos courtesy of Maria Bonazounta, Greek Consulate, Boston, Mass.

STEP ONE

Directions: Read the following story carefully.

Tony is a good-looking young man who, after graduating from high school, began working for a medium-sized department store. He is very intelligent and ambitious and recently was promoted to the position of assistant buyer for the store.

One evening when Tony was attending a party given by some of the employees from the store, he met Carlotta, a young woman who recently began working at the store as a secretary after graduating from college. Tony did not find anything special about Carlotta at first; but after one of his friends told him that her father was the president of the department store, he has suddenly become more interested in her.

At work Tony makes a point of saying hello to Carlotta every day and once in a while brings her a flower or asks her to have lunch with him. Carlotta finds it flattering to go with Tony since he is such a good-looking man, but she doesn't have any real serious intentions towards him in the beginning, since she knows her parents want her to marry someone from her own social class.

But, as time goes along, Tony's frequent invitations to go someplace, as well as his occasional little gifts to her, begin to influence Carlotta's way of thinking. Gradually she begins to reject her parents' wishes to marry within her own social class. Tony is not madly in love with Carlotta, but he feels that their marriage would be successful since he has confidence in himself.

Univ. students want love marriages, survey shows

The majority of . . . students of both sexes want love marriages. In choosing . . . mates, they think . . . most important . . . are love, *personality and health, in that order . . .*

(Excerpt from article in *Asahi Evening News*–Japan. June 28, 1976)

STEP TWO

Directions: When two people get married, there are a lot of things to consider. Based on the information in the story, decide what you think Tony and Carlotta consider important in choosing a spouse. Rank the following items from the most important to the least important, according to Tony's and Carlotta's feelings. Put number 1 for the most important, 2 for the next, etc.

	Tony	*Carlotta*
Love	_____	_____
Responsibility	_____	_____
Wealth 여흥	_____	_____
Looks	_____	_____
Personality	_____	_____
Social position 사회:위치	_____	_____
Family's advice	_____	_____
Health	_____	_____

Arranged Marriages.————The majority of marriages throughout the world are arranged and partners do not do the choosing. In Africa, much of Europe and especially southeastern Europe, the near east and orient, arranged marriages predominate.

In countries with arranged marriages the most universal custom is that someone acts as an intermediary or go-between. . . . Young people in these countries accept the view that their families should make the marriage choice for them.

From "Marriage" in Encyclopaedia Britannica, *14th Ed. (1976), 14:928.*

Photo courtesy of French Embassy Press & Information Division, New York

ANN  LANDERS

Dear Ann Landers:

I am 35 years old, a housewife, and have three children. We have been married 18 years. Our eldest child is 13. My husband is European-born and does not believe that parents should go anywhere without their children. The two of us have never been out for one evening together in our entire married life.

Am I wrong to tell him I don't think this is fair to me? When I mentioned it a few times he said, "There will be plenty of time for us to go out together after the children are on their own." What about it? He's a good husband but

I—Feel Trapped

Dear Trapped:

According to my arithmetic you married this man when you were 17 years old. I'm betting he is several years your senior and has always considered you more of a child than a woman.

It is virtually impossible for a wife to change her husband's thinking about family life after 18 years — especially if it's part of his cultural heritage. You might attempt a breakthrough by asking a close relative to babysit on your next wedding anniversary or birthday—whichever comes first. And good luck. I hope it works.

Ann Landers, Field Newspaper Syndicate.

STEP THREE

Directions: Break up into groups and discuss the analysis of Tony's and Carlotta's feelings that you made in Step Two. Use specific sentences from the story to support your analysis. Be sure to base your analysis on the information in the story and not on your personal opinions about choosing a spouse.

STEP FOUR

Directions: Now think about your own feelings concerning what is important in choosing a spouse. Rank the items below from the most important to least important. Do this by yourself.

Love	3
Responsibility	2
Wealth	X
Looks	7
Personality	1
Social position	6
Family's advice	5
Health	4

STEP FIVE

Directions: Discuss in your group your individual feelings about what you consider important in choosing a spouse.

ADDITIONAL EXERCISES

1. Write an essay about what you consider important in choosing a spouse.
2. What do you think might be some of the problems which a couple of different races, religions, nationalities or social classes would encounter in your society?

3. What do you imagine would be the advantages or disadvantages of an arranged marriage?

   or

   Do you think that arranged marriages stabilize society and, if so, is that more important than an individual's right to choose his/her own spouse?
4. Write a reply to the letter written to Ann Landers.
5. Write a dialog in which you are talking to one of your friends about how you are going to tell your parents that you plan to marry a person of a different culture or nationality.

Studying a Foreign Language

2

One of the most important attitudinal factors [in learning a foreign language] is the attitude of the learner to [toward] the language and to [toward] its speakers.
—Bernard Spolsky/Wallace E. Lambert: *Language Learning,* Vol. XIX, 1969.

I wonder what I said?

> **A PERSON LEARNS A LANGUAGE BETTER WHEN HE WANTS TO BE A MEMBER OF THE GROUP SPEAKING THAT LANGUAGE.**
> —Bernard Spolsky: *Language Learning,* Vol. XIX, 1969.

STEP ONE

Directions: Read the following story carefully.

Edward is entering a university and has to decide what foreign language to study, since he needs 12 credit hours to graduate. He studied Spanish in high school and even had a chance to use some of it when he took a trip to Mexico one summer. He enjoyed his trip very much and thought that maybe some day he would like to work for an international company based in Latin America.

The reason the university requires students to study a foreign language is because they feel that it makes the students more sophisticated and educated. Edward does not feel that this should be the main reason for studying a foreign language. He thinks that being able to communicate with people from different cultures is far more important than just impressing people with your knowledge.

After considering the possibilities of studying German or French so that he could travel in Europe with little difficulty, he

Legal Assistant

Oil/Gas Industry

Is the British exploration and production subsidiary of one of the world's largest oil companies. We are now well advanced in the development of the Frigg gas field in the North Sea. We are looking for a qualified lawyer to augment our Legal Department. You would be based in Paris to advise on all legal aspects of our operations, especially those connected with the contractual requirements – plant, equipment, men, money and materials – concerned in the development of the

Paris

the, Company's practice and current systems; responsibility for drawing up the final contracts for signature. You would also be called upon to investigate the legal aspects of UK and other countries' taxation and insurance, laws of tort, security, and the laws of employment.
In addition to your salary, we provide accommodation, a realistic bonus scheme, life assurance, BUPA and four weeks' holiday.

You should have a law de
barrister or solicitor. Spoken French is a great advantage, or you should be ready – and able – to learn it quickly.

the Project Engineer in

Accounting and System

Tehran to £10,000 + excellent benefit

Our client, a major Development Bank in Tehran, is ex rapidly and is looking for experienced people to join th three year contracts. The bank has a number of accoun vacancies, notab Auditor and Financi
These are bo ew appointments ing full scope to
initiative creativity with technical possess a re
+, must speak fluent Farsi and with UK expe gained id

INDUSTRIAL DOCTOR

Required to head up the Medical Facili on an Oil Refinery in

NORTH AFRICA

Candidate must be fully conversant wit treatment of industrial accidents and be pared to and first-aid.

Applicants should be able to read an Arabic.

We can offer a marrie s paid) which

Managing Age

CONTRACTING

Our Client, an International Petro-Chemical contractor is se man to manage their permanent office in Algeria. He will maintai liaison with Government departments to preserve the company's represent their interests and provide a full service to "up cou construction

ALGIERS

The ma ppointed must have:
Near fluency in French.
Overseas experience

EUROPEAN APPLICATIONS ENGINEER

with responsibility for supporting our distributors on the Continent of Europe. This is an important position and reports to the European General Manager. Applicants should be qualified engineers, with ledge of computer interfaces and elec circuitry. pared to trave in s support an he Continent. A knowledge of European langu ges would be an advantage, but is not essentia benefits commensurate wit

Senior Management Consultants

Full reelance needed for U.K. and
signments.
ust have full command of at least French or talian, and be:
— Earning £7,500 per year
ced degree in business, management science, economics or engineering.
— Five-year management consulting experience, or
equivalent. in one or more of the following

QUALITY CONTROL INSPECTORS wanted
for foreign su
Bilingua
desirable
mechar
electri
chemi
positi
perio
and
C.P.
pli

European Investiga

ondon-based

A recently qualified Ch
a good knowledge of at le
– French or German, pr
with some experience
manufacturing and mark

Management Ac
and Deputy Cont

OVERSEAS

A key appointment in the overseas operations of a maj electronics company.
A qualified accountant, either ACA, ACCA or ACMA managerial ability and experience in post of Man
comp ities will employing some 3,000+ people in Portug cial actions according to the preparation of budgets, fo rrective actions needed.
Candidates should preferably possess a sound working know anguage training will be provided if necessary. Preferred age ent will be on ex-patriate terms including gener ctive to those curre

stocks and bonds

In your late 20s, early 30s?
With a good degree, preferably in Business Administration
Most likely 'international' by upbringing or birth. For example, you may have been educated first at Oxford, and then at the Sorbonne. Fluent in English, of course; and, ideally, in one or two other lan as well.

or a similar sales envir
Could this be you! If s
should be a place for yo
international Account E
London. After six month
raining you will become
h provid
with exc

ernational
mmunications
al Consultants

, one of the world's largest
nsulting firms, seeks several
essionals to join its expanding
ions consulting activities.
cies are available in European
the Middle East.
seek should have thorough
nce in one or several of the

:

neering

ngineering (Cable and
rience are essential.
nce would be helpful)

gineering

tions hardware and

gement

sults administration

Senior PR Executive
Up to £6000 – Spain

Due to ex
o
Executive to be based in Spain.
Applicants, probably aged around 30, must be fluent in both Spanish
and English, and have several years experience in all aspec
relations – some of which should have included c
Self-motivation, diplomacy, writing
and the
qualities. A knowledge of travel or a related industry could prove a
distinct advantage.
Considerable travel throughout Spain and the rest of Europe is
envisaged, as well as to England where regular contact will be
maintained.
In addition to a salary of up to £6000 pa. an attractive range of
benefits apply.
Please write with brief detail

established,
either as
l companies or as con-
ssential, and French or
able asset.

tions

ally
tered Accountant with
east one foreign language
eferably both, and also
stigations, is offe
ting group.
he investigations on

cessful candidate will be experienced in all import/export
matters, custom's negotiations, purchase negotiations
for export general office
work. Patience to learn will
be essential. Good starting
salary—modern office— excellent prospects—all social be

are invited to th
Please send English and Japa-
nese resume stating full business experience and pr
ity to Classif
Tokyo.
Your application will be
treated as strictly confiden-
tial.

REWRITER AND PROOF-
REWIER needed, native
of English. College

girls, some Engli
speaking. High salary. litt
after
1034. 10-6-38. 7-16. 3-chome.

anted by trade agency. Require
ome Engli h. Experience
Call

SECRETARY able to ty
gch or/and French well, want
part-time of
in Engli h and photo to Clas
At No. 2 9.
Tok

EXPERI CED MULTI-
GRAPH OPERA
TYPIST needed for inte
la ated i
hinagasaki)
English speaking
Excellent wor

ry to Ambassador, good
English knowledge is essen
Someone who has
em-
bassy is preferable. Good
working conditions and salary will be offered. Please
call Monday to Fri-
day, 10:00 a.m. to 2:00 p.m.

EMBASSY urgently
secre applicants should
eak/read French and Eng
Good typing
needed. English required.
Send resume to Classified Ad

ccountant
roller

r British communications and

with strong personal qualities,
pment is required to fill the
and tra
recasts and a wid
y making recommen
ledge of Portuguese,
range is 25-30.
us housing
year.

EXPORT MANAGER

xcellent opportu
ased C.E.M. We ar
les oriented expo
uses res or rela
ou d. Multi-lingua

WANTED BILINGUAL
SECRETARY
with good ability of writ
ten and spoken English.
Good salary and workin
ditions for su
Apply in writ-
ing in English with re-
sume and photograph to

Room 702B Kyodo Bldg.
1-18, Nihonbashi Kayaba
cho, Chuo-ku, Tokyo. A
plications close April 2.

The European Parliament
in Luxembourg

is organising an open competition, based on qualifications, experience
and tests, to fill any vacant posts and draw up a reserve list (valid until
31 December 1976) for

Assistant Translators
English language

Candidates, maxim

command of English:

thorough knowledge of two of the following languages – DANISH,
DUTCH, FRENCH, GERMAN, ITALIAN;

a university degree or at least five years' equiva professional

nment.
, there
u as an
ecutive in
s intensive

finally makes up his mind to continue his study of Spanish. He feels that a high level of proficiency in Spanish would make it much easier for him to be accepted socially and culturally if he decides to live in a Spanish-speaking country for some time.

STEP TWO

Directions: There are many different reasons why people study foreign languages. Based on the information in the story, decide what you think Edward's reasons are for studying a foreign language. Rank the following items from the most important to the least important, according to Edward's feelings. Put number 1 for the most important, 2 for the next, etc.

	Edward
To travel abroad	2
To get a job	2
To learn about another culture	4
To be accepted by the people of another culture or country	
To have something to do in his free time	5
To be more sophisticated and educated	6
To fulfill an educational (requirement)	1

STEP THREE

Directions: Break up into groups and discuss the analysis of Edward's feelings that you made in Step Two. Use specific sentences from the story to support your analysis. Be sure to base your analysis on the information in the story and not on your personal opinions about studying foreign languages.

STEP FOUR

Directions: Now think about what reasons *you* consider important for studying a foreign language. Rank the items below from most important to least important. Do this by yourself.

To travel abroad	3
To get a job	2
To learn about another culture	4
To be accepted by the people of another culture or country	
To have something to do in your free time	1
To be more sophisticated and educated	5
To fulfill an educational requirement	6

STEP FIVE

Directions: Discuss in your group your individual opinions about what you consider important or good reasons for studying a foreign language.

LEARNING A SECOND LANGUAGE IS A KEY TO POSSIBLE MEMBERSHIP OF A SECONDARY SOCIETY: THE DESIRE TO JOIN THAT GROUP IS A MAJOR FACTOR IN LANGUAGE LEARNING.

—Bernard Spolsky: *Language Learning,* Vol. XIX, 1969.

ADDITIONAL EXERCISES

1. Do you think some people can learn languages more easily than others? If so, what factor or factors do you think make the difference?

2. Write a paragraph or two explaining why you are studying English.

3. What are the advantages in your country of being able to speak more than one language?

4. Explain how you think your parents, friends, and neighbors would feel if you spoke English fluently.

5. Read through the job ads. Can you think of other types of jobs in which a knowledge of one or more foreign languages is useful?

Selecting a Job or Position in a Company

3

STEP ONE

Directions: Read the following story carefully.
  Sam is studying welding in a two-year technical school and is about to graduate. He has had several job interviews: one with a big automobile company, one with a small company specializing in the construction of metal storage tanks, and one with an oil exploration company. The three jobs are quite different, but each one offers some advantages.

  Sam is only 20 years old and does not have any intentions of getting married right away. Since he has not had many chances to travel, he thinks it might be interesting to take the job with the oil exploration company. But his father has pointed out to him that the future of such a job is not very certain. Sam is aware of that fact, but the starting pay is about twice that of the other two jobs.

  The job with the small company also looks attractive, since it offers a lot of possibilities for advancement and would give him the chance to assume some direct responsibility which he would like to be able to do. He also feels it would be a very rewarding job but is not certain whether he is ready to be tied down in one place.

His father has tried to persuade him to take the job with the auto company, since it offers lots of benefits and a fairly high degree of security. Sam is afraid, however, that working on an assembly line would be rather boring and would not give him a chance to assume any responsibility on the job. He finally decides to join the oil exploration company.

STEP TWO

Directions: When people select a job or career, there are many different points to consider. Based on the information in the story, decide what you think Sam considers important in selecting a job. Rank the following items from the most important to the least important, according to Sam's feelings. Put number 1 for the most important, 2 for the next, etc.

	Sam
Pay	_____
Social prestige	_____
Security and benefits	_____
Freedom of movement	_____
Opportunity for advancement	_____
Personal satisfaction	_____
Level of responsibility (rank one)	
(*a*) requires a lot	_____
(*b*) requires little or none	_____
Social usefulness	_____

STEP THREE

Directions: Break up into groups and discuss the analysis of Sam's feelings that you made in Step Two. Use specific sentences

SITUATIONS (MALE OR FEMALE)

BAKERY ASSISTANT

wanted, 6 a.m. start.

BLOCKLAYERS wanted for large contract Blandford/ Dorchester area. Contact— anytime. 2/TA7

2/C

Broadwey County Secondary School Broadwey Weymouth

TEACHER OF HISTORY AND CIVICS

required from the beginning of term (January 12). This is a temporary appointment and involves teaching these subjects up to 'O' level Applicants please contact:

HEADMASTER (as soon as possible) UPWE

Famous Dorset country inn with unique dining room and excellent kitchen facilities require:

EXPERIENCED AND VERSATILE CHEF

well trained in the preparation of good traditional country fare. This is not a position for a rolling stone, but an opportunity for a mature person seeking to carve out a permanent and well paid career. References essential

Please telephone:

CARPENTER required for second fix. Immediate start. —Tel. 2/C7

ENGINEERS LTD.

require

SKILLED CENTRE LATHE TURNER

TEL. WEYMOUTH 73613

2/TA8

HAIRSTYLIST

for

of Dorchester

Must be fully exper Permanent position. Saturday half-day Good remuneration.

WANTED, a full part-time assi grocery shop at Corner. Must and good at

WORKIN CHARGEH

CARPENTER/BR

for smaller co nent position. particulars of for int

SPARETIME workers wanted to work from home, good earnings. Write P.O. Box 8, ket Mail. Wallasey. Merseyside. Mar-
2/TA10
SUPERVISORY assistant required at Colfox School, Bridport, for 7½ hours a week, Monday to Friday. Wages £6.07. Free lunches. Applications to—The Headmaster, by January 14, 1976. 2/C8
TWO skilled bricklayers required. Albany Road, Granby Industrial Estate. Weymouth 71422. 2/C7

REPRESENTATIVES AND AGENTS

WINDOWS

have a vacancy for a SALES REPRESENTATIVE in the Weymouth area. Exhibition caravan

Imr Ful

Bo

MANAGERESS /Manager required by Curtis, the Bakers, for their Dorchester branch. Previous experience in busy shop essential, pleasant manner, sales ability and good references are required for this vacancy. Top wages after trial period. — Tel. Weymouth 75156 for interview. 2/C9

PERSON required to manage old established men's outfitters. — Tel. Dorchester 2575. 2 C9

PANEL beater required for our busy car and light commercial body repair shop. Overtime available, good wages and bonus. — Apply

PERSON required for milk round, experience preferred with reference. Apply 2/C8

SALES representative required, need not have previous experience, but must want to sell, to take over an established 'Home Service' Insurance Agency covering the Dorchester area. While there is a sound basic salary plus an allowance towards travelling expenses, the commission and bonus elements are first-class. Earnings are therefore related to individual effort and sales ability but we would expect a satisfactory representative to earn at the rate of £3,000 plus a year. Promotions come from Agency level. Excellent pension and sick pay scheme. For appointment in strict confidence — Tel. Dorchester 2949. District Manager.

areas. Part-o work with in company. ass reproduc- High earn- to buy. No needed. Age Must have use —Tel. Wey- 2/TA7

TYRE SERVICES

Regional Tyre Services) equire the services of a

CLEANER their modern offices in NCE OF WALES ROAD hours per week. £1.50.

Please Tel.

Application for Employment

A division of ▮▮▮▮ Corporation

EQUAL OPPORTUNITY EMPLOYER

DATE APPLIED

NAME - PLEASE PRINT - LAST, FIRST, MIDDLE,

CURRENT ADDRESS - ADDRESS, CITY, STATE, ZIP

PRIOR ADDRESS - ADDRESS, CITY, STATE, ZIP

SOC. SEC. NUMBER

IF NOT U.S. CITIZEN PROVIDE VISA NUMBER

HOME TELEPHONE NUMBER

WHO SHOULD BE NOTIFIED IN CASE OF EMERGENCY?

(NAME) (PHONE) (RELATIONSHIP)

IF YES TO ANY OF THE FOUR QUESTIONS, PLEASE EXPLAIN:

HAVE YOU BEEN REFUSED BOND? NO ☐ YES ☐

HAVE YOU BEEN CONVICTED OF A FELONY OR MISDEMEANOR? NO ☐ YES ☐

HAVE YOUR WAGES EVER BEEN GARNISHED WITHIN THE LAST 7 YRS.? NO ☐ YES ☐

HAVE YOU FILED BANKRUPTCY IN THE LAST 14 YRS.? NO ☐ YES ☐

NAME OF HIGH SCHOOL.

ADDRESS GRADE COMPLETED DATE COMPLETED

ADVANCED EDUCATION

ADDRESS YEAR COMPLETED DATE

POSITION(S) DESIRED

☐ FULL TIME ☐ PERMANENT
☐ PART TIME ☐ TEMPORARY

DAYS AND HOURS AVAILABLE

WAGE DESIRED:

FORM 995 (1/75)

PREVIOUS EMPLOYMENT RECORD   *(List most recent employer first, if none list reference other than relatives.)*

IF CURRENTLY EMPLOYED ☐ Yes ☐ No   MAY WE CONTACT YOUR PRESENT EMPLOYER ☐ Yes ☐ No

COMPANIES	DATES	POSITION(S)	WAGE	WHY LEFT
1. CO. NAME	FROM	START	START	
CO. ADDRESS	TO	FINAL	FINAL	
CO. PHONE NUMBER	SUPERVISOR(S)			
2. CO. NAME	FROM	START	START	
CO. ADDRESS	TO	FINAL	FINAL	
CO. PHONE NUMBER	SUPERVISOR(S)			
3. CO. NAME	FROM	START	START	
CO. ADDRESS	TO	FINAL	FINAL	
CO. PHONE NUMBER	SUPERVISOR(S)			

MILITARY SERVICE
BRANCH _____

RANK _____   FROM _____ START _____ TYPE OF DISCHARGE

                         TO _____ FINAL _____

HAVE YOU EVER BEEN
EMPLOYED BY ▓▓▓▓ ?   WHAT STORE?   WHAT DEPT.?

LIST ALL FRIENDS AND RELATIVES
EMPLOYED AT ▓▓▓▓. (Specify Store Location)

IMPORTANT: READ BEFORE SIGNING!

I understand and agree that; (a) any false statement on this application will be cause for dismissal, (b) I will abide by the policies of ▓▓▓ as a condition of my employment, (c) I will be bonded, (d) reference investigations may be made regarding my credit status, character and work record as it relates to my employment.

SIGNATURE _____

from the story to support your analysis. Be sure to base your analysis on the information in the story and not on your own personal opinions about selecting a job.

STEP FOUR

Directions: Now think about your own feelings concerning what is important in selecting a job. Rank the items below from most important to least important. Do this by yourself.

Pay   ————

Social prestige ————

Security and benefits ————

Freedom of movement ————

Opportunity for advancement ————

Personal satisfaction ————

Level of responsibility (rank one)

 (*a*) requires a lot ————

 (*b*) requires little or none ————

Social usefulness ————

STEP FIVE

Directions: Discuss in your group your individual opinions about what you consider important in selecting a job.

ADDITIONAL EXERCISES

1. Write an essay explaining your personal feelings about what you consider important factors in selecting a job. You may want to add some factors or ideas that were not mentioned in the case study.

Photo courtesy of Royal Danish Ministry for Foreign Affairs, Copenhagen, Denmark

People in the countries listed were asked: *Why do you think a man works?*
Here are their answers:

	to earn money	to do his duty as a member of society	to find self-fulfillment
Japan	54%	12%	34%
USA	58%	12%	30%
UK	80%	6%	14%
West Germany	70%	13%	17%
France	80%	5%	15%
Switzerland	62%	16%	22%
Sweden	75%	8%	17%
Yugoslavia	70%	23%	7%
Philippines	54%	22%	24%
India	53%	20%	27%
Brazil	43%	14%	43%

is progressing well. My advisor is satisfied with my thesis so far, so it looks like I'll be graduating by the end of the year.

And in connection with that, you remember I mentioned to you that I had gotten a couple of good - almost unbelievably good - job offers here. The prospect for a good job at home, in my field, are poor. The visa problem can be handled easily and the job would be valuable experience for me as well as giving me a chance to save money. So I've decided to work here in the States for several years. After that, I don't know what I'll do. Mother will be disappointed - try to explain to her. I'll give you all the details in the next letter.

Please give my greetings to everyone at home.

Your Son

2. Look at the statistics on page 27. How would you interpret the meaning of the graph? Is your country listed there? Why do you think most people in your country work? What about you?

3. Read the letter from the foreign student to his father. Discuss how you think the foreign student feels. How do you think his parents feel? Write the answer to his letter which you think his father might send him. Write a dialog between the father and mother in which the father tells her that their son is going to get a job in the States.

4. Look at the job ads on pages 20 and 23. What are the qualities or benefits of each job that make it attractive to different types of people? Which of the jobs is most appealing to you and why? Role play a job interview for that job.

Advanced

Education

4

Photo courtesy of Lee Lindquist, Boston

> You send your child to the school master, but it is the school-boys who educate him. You send him to the Latin class, but much of his tuition comes, on his way to school from the shop-windows.
>
> —Emerson: *Conduct of Life.* "Culture," p. 193

STEP ONE

Directions: Read the following story carefully.

Irene is in her last year of high school and is considering whether to continue her education after graduation. She is a fairly good student and has always been encouraged by her parents to study hard so that she could get into the college of her choice. But she is beginning to get tired of studying all the time and is also beginning to question why she should continue her education. When she raised the question of whether or not she should continue studying, her parents were quite surprised and told her to think of all of her cousins and friends who were either already in college or would be going soon.

Irene does not know what to say to her parents after their discussion. She had once thought about becoming a nurse, since her favorite aunt is one. She also does not know what she will do if she does not go to college, since she doesn't want to get a job and work right away. She thinks that if she were to get a job she probably wouldn't be able to see her friends very often. She finally decides that, as long as her parents are willing to pay for everything, she should take advantage of the opportunity and enroll in a nursing program. After all, she thinks, it is always good for a woman to have some practical training or skill in case she has to work in the future.

> What we need is fewer overeducated, underskilled college graduates, and more people with solid technical and mechanical training.
>
> —An employer

STEP TWO

Directions: The number of high school graduates seeking some kind of advanced education (college, junior college, 2-year technical school) has been increasing in many countries around the world. There are many different reasons for this. Based on the information in the story, decide why you think Irene chose to continue her education after graduating from high school. Rank the following items from the most important to the least important, according to Irene's feelings. Put number 1 for the most important, 2 for the next, etc.

	Irene
To get a good job	_____
To satisfy her parents' wishes	_____
To be able to learn more about something she is interested in	_____
To kill time before getting a job or getting married	_____
Because it's the socially acceptable thing to do	_____
Because it's one step towards fulfilling a dream which Irene has had for a long time	_____
To continue to be with her friends and to have more freedom than she would have if she were working	_____
To have an education to fall back on in case she has to work in the future	_____

Practical = useful
willing = wants to do
take advantage of = make use of it
enroll =

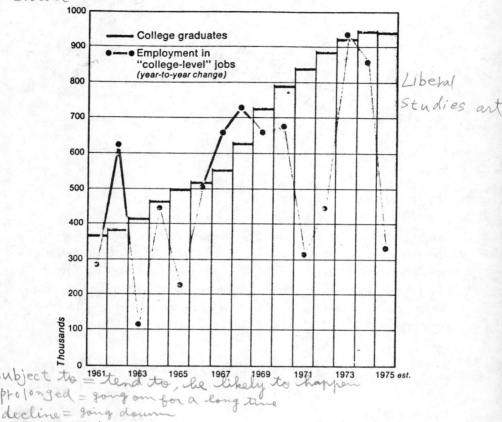

Subject to = tend to, be likely to happen
prolonged = going on for a long time
decline = going down
eliciting = get a response.

Liberal Studies art

A CHANGING MARKET FOR EDUCATED PRODUCTS

Until 1975, the nation's production of college graduates stepped up contin-
uously year after year. But the economy's demand for these new degree
holders has been subject to wide swings, dropping sharply in the last few
years. This prolonged decline is eliciting the classic response: in 1975, fewer
young people found it worthwhile to get a bachelor's degree.

Employment in "college-level" jobs fluctuates in part because of
destabilizing government policies. Demand is blown up when Congress votes
huge appropriations for programs, and collapses when the programs are
ended. Also, employment of college graduates is an economic indicator: dips
in "net new hires" were especially steep in bad economic years.

The definition of a "college-level" job includes those classified as "professional and technical" (e.g., doctors, lawyers, educators, and scientists) and as
"managerial and administrative," which takes in most executives and public
officials.

fluctuates = uneven = very
appropriation =

—*Fortune,* January 1976, p. 129

MASS EDUCATION FOR ALL, OR QUALITY EDUCATION FOR A FEW?

STEP THREE

Directions: Break up into groups and discuss the analysis of Irene's feelings that you made in Step Two. Use specific sentences from the story to support your analysis. Be sure to base your analysis on the information in the story and not on your personal opinions about reasons for seeking advanced education.

STEP FOUR

Directions: Now think about what reasons *you* consider important in seeking an advanced education. Rank the items below from most important to least important. Do this by yourself.

To get a good job   2

To satisfy your parents' wishes   _____

To be able to learn more about something
   you are interested in   1

To kill time before getting a job or getting
   married   _____

Because it's the socially acceptable thing to do   _____

Because it's one step towards fulfilling a dream
   which you have had for a long time   _____

To continue to be with your friends and to have
more freedom than you would have if you
were working

(For a woman) to have an education to fall
back on in case you have to work in the
future   3

STEP FIVE

Directions: Discuss in your group your individual opinions about what reasons you consider important in deciding to seek an advanced education.

> STUDENTS TURNING TO FARM STUDIES: Students preparing for college entrance examinations, . . . who would have flocked to engineering or law in the 1960s, are . . . taking a crack at . . . fields . . . animal husbandry, fisheries and dairy farming.

ADDITIONAL EXERCISES

1. What do you think is the meaning of the quote by Emerson on page 31?

2. Look at the picture of university students on page 30. Do you think a country should have as many college graduates as possible? Why do some people say that mass education is poor quality education?

3. Read the quote by the employer on page 32. What does he mean? Do you agree?

34 STATE UNIVERSITIES BEGIN TAKING STUDENT APPLICATIONS

The Education Ministry . . . estimates that 73 of . . . 100 aspirants will be admitted, *but only if they do not insist on universities of their first choice.* [Italics added]

Excerpt from *The Japan Times*, Feb. 3, 1976.

4. Whose responsibility do you think it is to pay educational expenses? If you're thinking of getting further education after high school, how do you plan to pay for it?

5. Look at the excerpt from a newspaper article above. What do you think the headline means?

6. Role play a situation in which a son/daughter is trying to convince his/her parents that it's important that he/she get an advanced education.

Childhood
Activities

5

Soviet mothers seem remarkably uninterested in preschool political socialization, moral education, or patriotic training. In a 1969 survey, 66.6 percent of the working mothers included in the sample indicated that they sent their young children to preschool facilities simply because there was no one else suitable to care for them. Only 23.7 percent indicated that they had enrolled their children primarily because they felt it would provide a better social upbringing than could be provided by another means (including the family).

Thus, for some time now, many of the stereotypes and dogged principles of preschool care have been undergoing a challenge through the publication of empirical research. The old givens are no longer simply articles of faith and the results have not been good enough in this process. Of course, the political and social goals of this initial socialization and education experience are also being reevaluated.

Susan Jacoby "Who Raises Russia's Children?" *Saturday Review*, Aug. 21, 1971. *Pol. Sci. Q.* 88:709, Dec. 1973. Copyright by The Academy of Political Science 1973.

STEP ONE

Directions: Read the following story carefully.

Bob is a thirteen year old whose favorite time of day is after school when he gets together with the other kids in his neighborhood to play baseball or ride around on their bikes. Although Bob's parents are glad to see that their son enjoys the company of the other boys and gets his daily dose of vigorous exercise, they are concerned that his school work may be suffering.

His parents are high school graduates but did not have a chance to go to college. Both of them are convinced that the road to a successful life passes through the college campus. Bob's father feels that, although he's competent in his job, the personnel manager usually passes him over and gives the promotions to college grads instead.

In order to help Bob avoid this same problem in the future, Bob's parents have been saving money since he was born so that he can get a college education. Now, in order to make sure he can

qualify for a good college, they have decided that Bob should study a little harder. Bob's parents plan to help him with his homework from now on until he learns to concentrate on his work and begins to understand the importance of studying.

In addition, Bob's father has advised his son to sign up for the school's track and field team. He feels that it will be a good change of pace from studying and at the same time provide Bob with training in discipline—both physical and mental.

STEP TWO

Directions: Based on the information in the story, decide what childhood activities you think Bob's parents consider to be important. Rank the following items from the most important to the least important. Put number 1 for the most important, 2 for the next, etc.

Children should —   *Bob's parents*
    study hard in order to have a good future
    have fun in order to enjoy their
        childhood   _____
    spend a lot of time with other children in
        order to learn about getting along
        socially   _____
    take lessons in extra things like music or
        sports in order to develop special skills   _____
    be physically active in order to develop
        their bodies
    have free time in order to discover their
        talents and interests   _____

STEP THREE

Directions: Break up into groups and discuss the analysis of Bob's parents' feelings that you made in Step Two. Use specific

Panel probes rising school crime. A staff report by the Senate Judiciary Subcommittee to Investigate Juvenile Delinquency, made public April 9, warned that increasing crime and an "unprecedented wave of wanton destruction and vandalism" were reaching "crisis proportions which seriously threaten the ability of our educational system to carry out its primary function" of teaching.

Sen. Birch Bayh (D, Ind.), the subcommittee's chairman, who began hearings April 16 on this problem, announced his intention to introduce a bill that would provide grants to states to help make schools safer. (Similar safe-school bills had been introduced in the previous two Congresses but had failed to pass, although funding for the National Institution of Education to report on such legislation by 1976 was approved in 1974.)

—Facts on File, Vol. 35, No. 1798, pp. 278-279

sentences from the story to support your analysis. Be sure to base your analysis on the information in the story and not on your personal opinions about what activities are good for children.

STEP FOUR

Directions: Now think about your own feelings concerning what activities are important for children. Rank the items below from the most important to the least important. Do this by yourself.

Children should —
    study hard in order to have a good future   ———
    have fun in order to enjoy their childhood   ———
    spend a lot of time with other children in
        order to learn about getting along
        socially   ———
    take lessons in extra things like music or
        sports in order to develop special skills   ———
    be physically active in order to develop
        their bodies   ———
    have free time in order to discover their
        talents and interests   ———

STEP FIVE

Directions: Discuss in your group your individual opinions about what activities are important for children.

ADDITIONAL EXERCISES

1. Write what you think Bob thinks about his parents' decision.
2. Do you think children should work in order to help their parents support the family if necessary? If so, at what age? Should they be paid at the same rate as adults?
3. Do you think parents should encourage a three or four year old child to begin studying something in order to try to speed up his or her mental development?
4. Write a dialog between a mother and her son or daughter in which the mother is trying to convince the child to begin studying the piano, violin or some other musical instrument.

5. Write a short essay about some unforgettable event in your childhood.

6. Why do you think some young people engage in such activities as damaging public property, stealing, or fighting? Have you ever witnessed, been a victim of, or engaged in any of these activities?

7. Generally speaking, in your country, what differences are there in the way boys and girls are raised—who they play with, acceptable activities, dress, education, etc.?

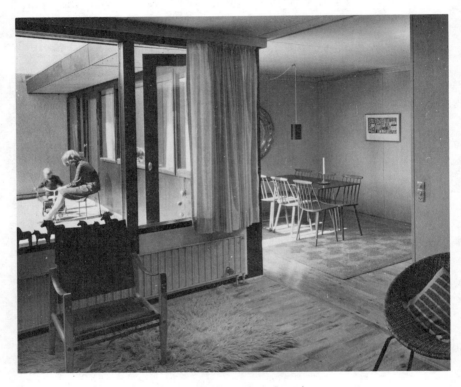

Photo courtesy Royal Danish Ministry for Foreign Affairs, Copenhagen, Denmark

Deciding
Where to Live

6

Cramped =
Conveniences =
atmosphere =
anti-pollution =
environmental pollution =
affected =
relatively =

"Pushers" help commuters get to work on time.

STEP ONE

Directions: Read the following story carefully.

Anna and Herman are a young married couple with two small children. They live in a large city in a small apartment that has become too cramped for their growing family. They are thinking about moving to a bigger place, but they haven't decided yet if they should find a place in the city, move to the suburbs, or go out to the country to live.

Anna was raised in the city and likes the conveniences and lively atmosphere of city life, especially the educational, cultural and social opportunities. Herman, on the other hand, likes the advantages of the friendly small town life that he knew as a boy when he had plenty of space and opportunities to enjoy the countryside. During the week, Herman works long hours for an accounting firm downtown. Anna is busy taking care of their children, but she also finds time to attend art classes twice a month and weekly meetings of a local anti-pollution organization. Weekends they devote to pleasure. Sometimes they go out for dinner and a concert with their friends who also live in the city. Sometimes they take their children for a picnic and hiking, to a park, or to swim or play tennis. However, they both feel that the good recreation areas are all too far away, and they have to spend a lot of time just getting there. The parks near their house, on the other hand, are crowded and affected by the increasing noise and environmental pollution of the city.

Anna generally dislikes the idea of moving into the country, except that she would like them to own their own home and that would be made possible by the relatively low real estate values there. Herman would gladly move to the countryside, except that he dislikes the idea of spending so much time commuting to and from his office.

Population statistics, trends. The world's population passed 4 billion April 1, according to Dr. L. C. Nehrt, a Wichita State University professor and consultant to the United Nations. He based his figures on current U.N. data including a growth rate of 2.05 per cent annually.

The population migration to U.S. cities had been halted or reversed, it was reported Feb. 9. U.S. Census Bureau figures showed that in the 15 largest metropolitan centers, more people had moved out than in, but the population increased slightly because births had exceeded deaths. The trend was to towns of less than 10,000 people and to rural living, according to Calvin Beale, head of population studies for the U.S. Agriculture Department. He cited as reasons: an improved economy in smaller towns; fear of the city, particularly among parents; and a desire, particularly among younger people, to return to a more natural environment.

Photo courtesy of The Gloucester Daily Times, *Gloucester, Mass.*

STEP TWO

Directions: Break into groups and analyze Anna and Herman's situation together. They have three choices: to live in the city, in the suburbs, or in the country. On a sheet of paper, list all the advantages and disadvantages for Anna and Herman of each of the three choices. Use specific sentences from the story to support your analysis.

STEP THREE

Directions: Based on the group's analysis of Anna and Herman's situation in Step Two, discuss what you think Anna and Herman will decide to do. Be careful to base your discussion on their situation and not on your own feelings.

STEP FOUR

Directions: Now think about your own feelings concerning what is important in deciding where to live. If you had a good job in a city and had the choice of deciding where to live, what points would you consider when making your decision? Rank the following items from the most important to the least important. Put number 1 for the most important, 2 for the next, etc.

The time it takes to get to work _____

Opportunities for entertainment and cultural
    activities _____

The cost of housing and food _____

Opportunities for and quality of education   _/_

A quiet and clean environment   _ᒣ_

The amount of space you would have to live
in and move around in outside   _____

The kind of neighbors you would have   _____

The conveniences of living (shopping,
availability of goods, services, material
comforts)   _____

THE 12 LARGEST CITIES IN THE WORLD
(millions of inhabitants)

1970		1985	
1. New York	16.3	Tokyo	25.2
2. Tokyo	14.9	New York	18.8
3. London	10.5	Mexico City	17.9
4. Shanghai	10.0	Sao Paulo	16.8
5. Mexico City	8.4	Shanghai	14.3
6. Los Angeles	8.4	Los Angeles	13.7
7. Buenos Aires	8.4	Bombay	13.7
8. Paris	8.4	Calcutta	12.1
9. Sao Paulo	7.8	Peking	12.0
10. Osaka	7.6	Osaka	11.8
11. Moscow	7.1	Buenos Aires	11.7
12. Peking	7.0	Rio de Janeiro	11.4

This data shows the twelve largest cities in the world in 1970, with their projected populations in 1985, and the twelve fastest growing cities, whose population will more than double by 1985. The data given here are based on a recent study of the U.N. Population Division entitled "The World's Million Cities, 1970-1985."

THE 12 FASTEST GROWING CITIES IN THE WORLD
(% of increase)

			1970	1985
			(millions of inhabitants)	
1.	Bandung	242	1.2	4.1
2.	Lagos	186	1.4	4.0
3.	Karachi	163	3.5	9.2
4.	Bogota	146	2.6	6.4
5.	Baghdad	145	2.0	4.9
6.	Bangkok	137	3.0	7.1
7.	Teheran	132	3.4	7.9
8.	Seoul	124	4.6	10.3
9.	Lima	121	2.8	6.2
10.	Sao Paulo	115	7.8	16.8
11.	Mexico City	113	8.4	17.9
12.	Bombay	109	5.8	12.1

STEP FIVE

Directions: Discuss in your group your individual opinions about what is important in deciding where to live.

ADDITIONAL EXERCISES

1. Write a dialog in which a young person (eighteen or older) is telling his/her parents why he/she is going to move to the city.
2. Whose responsibility do you think it is to provide good transportation for commuters working in big cities? What kind of transportation system do you think is the most practical and suitable for your country? Why?
3. Write a paragraph telling how you get to school or work, and how long it takes.
4. Do you think the government should control the size of cities and the distribution of people throughout the country, or should people have a free choice of living anywhere they want?
5. If you had a choice of living anywhere you wanted, what kind of place would it be? Write a paragraph or two describing it.
6. In your country, do people move often? Where do they move and for what reasons?

Deciding
How to Buy

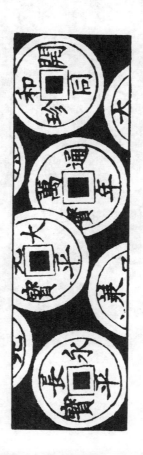

7

STEP ONE

Directions: Read the following story carefully.

Sophia and Hector are a middle-aged couple who will soon be celebrating their 25th wedding anniversary. Hector would like to buy something special for his wife and has been putting aside a little money each month over the past year. Being a hard-working, practical man, Hector thinks it might be nice to buy something for the house, since Sophia has been asking him for the past few years to buy a new rug for the living room. A couple of weeks ago, Hector told Sophia about his plan and asked her to go with him to the store to pick out the rug she would like. He told her that he had been able to save $400 and that she could spend up to that amount.

They go to the store and, after looking around for some time, Sophia finally sees a beautiful flowered rug that would be just perfect for their house. She asks how much it is, and the salesman tells her that it's $600. Hector frowns a little and asks the salesman if they have anything similar to it for around $400. The salesman shows them another rug which is about the same design, but the colors are not nearly as vivid and the quality of the material is not as good. Hector can easily see the difference between the two rugs, but only has $400.

At this point, Hector doesn't know exactly what to do. He had planned on only spending $400, and had to work hard to save that much over the past year. He has never believed in borrowing money except for some emergency. Sophia tells him how much she really likes the $600 rug and says that $200 isn't that much more since this will probably be the last rug they buy. Hector asks Sophia where she thinks he is going to get the additional $200. She suggests that, if he really doesn't want to borrow money and pay interest, they can take the $200 out of their savings account and pay it back later.

Hector says that to pay back the money may be easier said than done and asks her if she really thinks the cheaper rug looks that bad. After discussing the matter in more detail, Sophia smiles at Hector and tells him that, since it is his gift to her, she will gladly accept his decision. What do you think Hector will decide to do?

STEP TWO

Directions: Break into groups and analyze Hector's situation together. There are several different courses of action which Hector could take. Think about his character and decide what you think he is going to do. Use specific sentences from the story to support your analysis. Be sure to base your discussion on the information in the story and not on your own feelings.

STEP THREE

Directions: Now decide what you would do if you were in Hector's situation. Discuss your individual opinions with the members of your group.

PLEASE DIRECT ANY INQUIRY TO

DATE Mo. Day	Reference Number	TYPE OF TRANSACTION	MERCHANDISE CASH PRICE Including any tax and shipping charge	AMOUNT FINANCED Unpaid Balance of Cash Price	ADDED FOR FINANCE CHARGE	ANNUAL PERCENTAGE RATE	CHARGES OR CREDITS	DEFERRED PAYMENT PRICE Cash Price plus amount added for Finance Charge
0825	GZ47	RETAIL SALE	77000	77000	30400	14.75%	107400	107400
0825	GZ47	RETAIL SALE	61000	61000	24400	14.75%	85400	85400
0825	GZ47	RETAIL SALE	61000	61000	24400	14.75%	85400	85400

_1990_

ACCOUNT NUMBER	BILLING DATE	PREVIOUS BALANCE	NEW BALANCE (TOTAL OF PAYMENTS)	DUE DATE	MONTHLY PAYMENT No. Amount		FINAL PAYMENT
200330343894	90276	i	278200	92776	60	4625	700

Unless an **ANNUAL PERCENTAGE RATE** is shown above and if the **FINANCE CHARGE** exceeds $5.00, the **ANNUAL PERCENTAGE RATES** are:

FOR EASY PAYMENT PURCHASES	FOR MODERNIZING CREDIT PLAN PURCHASES
The **ANNUAL PERCENTAGE RATE** is 20%	The **ANNUAL PERCENTAGE RATE** is 14.75%

Ownership of the merchandise listed above which has been identified in your sales slip remains in ▪▪▪▪ until paid for in full in accordance with your Easy Payment Plan —Modernizing Credit Plan Retail Installment Contract and Security Agreement. If you pay in full in advance, any unearned **FINANCE CHARGE** will be rebated under the Rule of 78.

STEP FOUR

Directions: Now think about what factors you consider important when deciding what things to buy. Rank the following items below from most important to least important. Do this by yourself.

	A rug	Clothing	A bicycle or car
Beauty	___	___	___
Price	___	___	___
Practical utility or usefulness	___	___	___
Whether it's fashionable	___	___	___
Prestige of the brand name	___	___	___
Longterm durability	___	___	___
Reliability of the service guarantee	___	___	___
Uniqueness	___	___	___

WARRANTY

To the original purchaser (or gift recipient) of this product for home use, the _____ warrants that any part of the product which proves to be defective in materials or workmanship within one year of the date of such purchase or receipt will be repaired or replaced, at our option, free of charge, if delivered prepaid to one of our Servicenters or authorized Service Stations.

This warranty does not cover damage resulting from accident, misuse or abuse, nor does it cover wear, scratching or discoloration of the double non-stick coating. This warranty covers products purchased and retained within the U.S.A., wherever you may live or even if you move..

This is your warranty.

SERVICE
Should your p' _____
_____-owned _____

Your _____ is fully guaranteed against defects of material and workmanship for one year.

Now a wor _____
service is _____
authorize _____
Compan _____
indeper _____
Pages _____
Small _____
*Ref _____
Dou _____

GUARANTEE

GUARANTEE. Your _____ Shaver is guaranteed against electrical and mechanical defects in mater _____ ne year ship. Repairs or parts replacement required a _____ rkman- will be made free of charge during this _____ 'efects cover damage caused by misus _____ es not voltage other than that st _____ it or lieu of any other w _____ is in required, sen _____ ce Service _____ ire

HOUSEHOLD REFRIGERATOR WARRANTY

1. If your new _____ Household Refrigerator fails because of a manufacturing defect within one year from the date of original purchase for use, _____ will repair the product at no charge to you. Both parts and service labor are included.

2. In addition, if the sealed refrigerating system in your new _____ Refrigerator fails within the second through fifth year from the _____ purchase for use because of a manufact _____ will repair the sealed refrig _____ to you. Both the parts of _____ and service labor are incl _____

This warranty applies to pro _____ home use within the U.S.A _____ damage by accident, misuse _____

Guaranteed to sprout. If not, send a 10¢ stamp with your name and address to: _____ Garden Grove, CA 92641. Patents, Patents Pending, Trademarks, and Copyright property of _____ Transplanting information underneath flap. _____ is look us up in the yellow _____

GUARANTEE CERTIFICATE

This _____ Staple Gun is guaranteed against defective materials or workmanship for a period of 90 days and will be repaired or replaced at our option, free of charge if defective, within the terms of our guarantee. This guarantee applies only if genuine _____ staples are used. On repairs caused by use _____ es, abuse, or by nor- _____ ce, we will make a _____ Phone r replacement parts _____ ... service charge. Re- _____ postage and insurance charges will be added to repair cost.

STEP FIVE

Directions: Discuss in your group your individual opinions about deciding how to buy different kinds of things. If your rankings are different in the three columns above, why do you think they are different?

ADDITIONAL EXERCISES

1. Write a paragraph or two describing the method of buying in your country (cash and carry, barter system, charging system, bargaining system, etc.).
2. Role play a situation where you are trying to return a pair of defective shoes which you bought just a few days before. You want your money back, but the salesman only wants to exchange the defective pair for a new pair.
3. Write your own guarantee of some product such as a cosmetic, drug, health drink, some kind of tool, food, etc.
4. Look at the cartoon on page 57. Who in the family do you think should control the money?

II Problem

Solving

Family
Togetherness

8

Census Bur survey repts that families headed by women make up 9.6% of all white families and 35% of all black families; repts that 14% of all Amer children under age 18 are being raised by their mothers, compared with 8% in '60; says there were 6.6-million families headed by women in '73, increase of 1-million since '70; shows white women heading families climbed from 4.2-million in '70 to 4.7-million in '73, while number of black women increased from 1.3-million in '70 to 1.8-million in '73; like period in '74 shows increase in white families from 9.1-9.6%, while black families show increase from 28-35% (S), Ag 8, 14:1

—*New York Times Index*, 1974, Vol. A–M

STEP ONE

Directions: Read the following story carefully. As you read it, put yourself into the position of either the father or one of the children in the family.

Your father is a skilled technician who works for a big manufacturing firm that has several plants in other parts of the country. His job pays well, and he has to work only five days a week, so that on weekends you are able to do things together as a family.

One day he comes home and tells everyone at the dinner table that he has been offered a new position in the company. His job would be to help supervise the installing of machinery in new plants and the pay is one third more than he is currently earning. The only drawback is that the family would either have to move every year and a half or two years, which would mean your making new friends and changing schools, or you would have to live alone with your mother during the weekdays while he is working. Even if you move, you probably wouldn't have as many chances as now to do things with him since he would be busy with his work. But the better pay would mean that you could live in a nicer house, have more spending money, and go to college, if you wanted to, without having to work or borrow money in order to pay the tuition.

Your father does not have to take the new position, but he feels that the experience from this position may some day lead to an even better position in the company. He wonders, though, whether the increase in pay and responsibility is more important than the time he should spend with you and the rest of the family.

What do you think he should do in this situation?

STEP TWO

Directions: Break up into groups and write down all of the alternatives you can think of. Discuss the advantages and disadvantages of each one.

1. The father accepts the new job, but, rather than moving the whole family, he comes home on weekends.

2.

3.

STEP THREE

Directions: Based on your group's discussion of the advantages and disadvantages of each alternative, rank the possible courses of action and discuss your reasons for your rankings with the members of your group.

STEP FOUR

Directions: Complete the sentences on page 69 by putting a check mark (✓) in one of the three boxes. This step represents your personal opinion, so do it by yourself.

	Extremely important	Important	Not so important
1. For a man, being promoted in his job is . . .	✓		
2. For a father, to live with his children is . . .	✓	✓	
3. For children, to have the chance to go to the same school each year is . . .			✓
4. For a family, to do things together regularly is . . .		✓	✓
5. For children, to be able to develop intimate relationships with friends is . . .		✓	✓
6. For a family, to be able to improve their standard of living is . . .	✓		
7. For a husband and wife to live together all the time is . . .		✓	

ikstri:mli 非常地

Extremely important

促進
pɹə́mout

"Single parent families" . . . are a way of life
for 1 of every 7 American children. Across
the nation, according to the U.S. Census
Bureau, 9 million children [below age 18]
are being raised by one parent—more than 8
million by mothers, 800,000 by fathers . . .

Extracted from article in *The New York Times*,
Dec. 3, 1974

Photo courtesy of French Embassy Press & Information Service, New York

Photo courtesy of French Embassy Press & Information Service, New York

STEP FIVE

Directions: In your group, discuss your individual opinions about the ideas in Step Four.

ADDITIONAL EXERCISES

1. What kinds of things does/did your family do together?
2. What do you think it would be like to be sent to a boarding school?
3. Role play a situation where a father or mother is asking his/her children what they would like to do on a Saturday or on some evening.
4. From the viewpoint of a child whose father was to be sent overseas to work, would you want him to take you and the rest of your family, or would you rather stay in your native country and continue your education there? As a father, would you take your children or your wife? As a wife, would you want to take your children, go by yourself, or stay with the children?

5. Describe the attitude in your culture towards the family (father, mother, children, aunts, uncles, grandparents) doing things together. Are there only certain members of the family who do things together, or does the whole family do things together?

6. Write an essay describing some special event or holiday in your country when the whole family gets together.

7. How important do you think it is for children to be raised by both parents? What role do you think the father should play in raising his children?

What to do
About Grandmother

9

[Handwritten notes: family oriented 射 = 3 generations 三代同堂.

Youth-oriented society.]

MANY SUICIDES REPORTED ON RESPECT FOR AGED DAY

Tragic suicides by aged persons were reported from across the country Monday when the nation celebrated Respect for the Aged Day, a national holiday.

In the city of . . . , a 76-year-old woman was found to have hanged herself in her room at about 2 a.m., her grandson reported to police.

The woman, . . . , had been suffering from tuberculosis and the hardening of the arteries in addition to the loss of eyesight, the grandson told police.

In the city of . . . , a neighbor visited a 78-year-old man's home at 9 a.m. to find that he had gassed himself. The man, . . . , had lived alone on pension since 1961 when his wife died.

In . . . , a farmer reported to police that his 68-year-old wife hanged herself in a shed Monday afternoon.

The woman, Mrs. . . . , was worried about her frail health and had often talked of loneliness in old age, according to the husband. *[handwritten: ↓weak]*

A person fishing in the sea off the city of . . . found the body of an aged woman drifting at 10:20 a.m. Monday. Police later identified the body as that of . . . , 92, of . . . , who had been missing since Friday. *[handwritten: ↓can't function]*

Her family members believe that she *[handwritten: negative]* was overwhelmed by pessimism because she was unable to receive pension from the city office due to some flaw in her papers on Wednesday.

A 66-year-old woman hanged herself in a room in her house in . . . , while her daughter-in-law was in another room.

The daughter-in-law, Mrs. . . . , told police that her mother-in-law, . . . , had been almost bed-ridden since 1973.

In . . . , an aged woman committed suicide by jumping onto the track of the . . . Line in . . . at 6:50 p.m.

She was identified as . . . , 68, of . . . . She was suffering from stomach trouble and lived with her son's family.

STEP ONE

Directions: Read the following story carefully.

Hal Bohlman, his wife Judy, and their three children live in a small apartment. Hal works in the income tax <u>division</u> of the government where he is a public information officer. Their children are now 12, 10 and 5 years old. Their plan is for Judy to return to work after their youngest child starts elementary school next year. They hope to save up enough money to buy a house, since they feel their present two bedroom apartment is much too crowded.

Last week, however, Judy's father died suddenly of a heart attack. They now have to decide what to do about Judy's mother, since Judy is the only child. Judy's father was the manager of a store in a large supermarket chain, so her mother will receive a <u>modest</u> but sufficient pension from the company. In addition, she will receive the money from her husband's life insurance and will continue to receive social <u>welfare</u> benefits from the government. In order to avoid <u>inheritance</u> taxes, her husband in his will left his <u>estate</u> to Judy with the <u>provision</u> that his wife would have use of it as long as she lived.

Judy realizes that it would probably be dangerous for her mother to live alone. Although her health is basically good for someone her age, 73, she has bad days when her heart or arthritis act up. Judy is afraid she might have trouble taking care of herself now that she is alone. She is living in the house that she and her husband owned, a three bedroom house in the suburbs of the same city where Hal and Judy live.

Hal and Judy's mother never got along well in the past, but Hal realizes that Judy is worried about her mother.

STEP TWO

Directions: Break up into groups. Read the possible courses of action that Judy and Hal thought of. As a group, add to this list other possible courses of action that you think of. At this time,

Photo courtesy of Italian Government Travel Office, New York

Photo courtesy of Royal Danish Ministry for Foreign Affairs, Copenhagen, Denmark

do not try to evaluate the suggestions; just try to list as many as you can.

1. They can put Judy's mother in a nursing home and move into her house.

2. They can hire a full-time housekeeper to live with Judy's mother.

3. They can ask grandmother what she wants to do.

4. They can try letting her live by herself in her own house for a while to see if her health would permit such a solution.

5. They can sell her house, put her in a nice nursing home, and buy a house for themselves.

6.

7.

Extracts from news articles about nursing homes—

The ———— Nursing Home is providing substandard patient care, according to state officials, and the home will be given two weeks to improve conditions or face decertification and license revocation. . . .

Violations uncovered . . . include poor patient grooming and a lack of patient care.

State inspectors went into the home on an anonymous telephone call . . . and found "the kitchen dirty and the whole place dirty at that time." That's when the patient care problems were also uncovered.

STEP THREE

Directions: In your group, look over the total list of suggestions in Step Two. Talk about the advantages and disadvantages of each of them. Try to decide which course of action you think Hal and Judy should take.

STEP FOUR

Directions: Give your opinion about the sentences on page 79 by putting a check mark in one of the three boxes. This step represents your personal opinion, so do it by yourself.

	Yes	No	Not necessarily
1. For a family to live in its own house and have a lot of space is important.	☐	☐	☐
2. An older person living alone would be lonely, and such a situation should be avoided 避免 包.	☐	☐	☐
3. A nursing home is more qualified and better kwɔlifaid 限制 equipped to care for an older person than that person's family is.	☐	☐	☐
4. Children should take care of their parents 财政上 financially (pay medical bills, nursing home fees, etc.).	☐	☐	☐
5. Children should take care of their parents themselves (live with them).	☐	☐	☐
6. It is better for young parents and their seperet 分开 children to live separate from grandparents.	☐	☐	☐
7. The happiness of a young family is more important than the happiness of an old grandparent.	☐	☐	☐

STEP FIVE

Directions: In your group, discuss your individual opinions about the ideas in Step Four.

ADDITIONAL EXERCISES

1. Write an essay on one of the following:
   (*a*) What you would do in Hal and Judy's situation.
   (*b*) Any of the ideas in Step Four.
2. Read the news article on page 74. Why do you think this kind of lonely death occurs? What are the causes?
3. Do you think nursing homes are a good way to take care of old people? Are there nursing homes in your country?
4. What kind of life style do you hope or expect to have when you are old?
5. Would you like your grandparents or parents to live with you when they are old?
6. In your country, what kind of life style and social position do old people have?

Neighborliness

10

Good Fences

MAKE

Good Neighbors

STEP ONE

Directions: Read the following story carefully. As you read it, put yourself into the story and consider what you would do if you were faced with this situation.

You and your family have been living in the same six-family apartment building for eight years. The landlord's family also lives there, and generally speaking all the tenants get along fairly well with each other. Recently, however, there was a change in the apartment next to yours.

A nice, quiet old couple used to live there. The old lady would sometimes bring over some cookies or small cakes she had made, and your mother in return would give them some food or help the old woman with her shopping. Unfortunately, the old lady died last month. Her husband couldn't live alone, so his grandson moved in with him.

The grandson, who is about twenty, has become a problem to your family. The walls of the building are thin and he is noisy. You are used to peace and quiet, but the grandson likes to listen to his radio late at night. Sometimes friends of his visit, and they make a lot of noise. Everyone in your family is bothered by your new neighbor and as a result is becoming more irritated.

Your mother once politely asked the old man if he was able to sleep well at night, but apparently he didn't get the hint. If he did understand your mother's intention and did speak to his grandson about it, the grandson apparently didn't listen, since things haven't changed any. Everyone in your family agrees that something has to be done, but no one wants to hurt the old man's feelings or cause him any problems.

What do you think should be done?

STEP TWO

Directions: Break up into groups. Read the possible courses of action below. As a group, add to this list other possible courses of action that you can think of. At this time do not try to evaluate the suggestions; just try to think of as many as you can.

1. The family could try to ignore the noise and hope the grandson will realize that his behavior is bothering other people.
2. One of the parents could talk to the old man since they know him.
3. When the neighbor is noisy the family could pound on the wall and not say anything.
4.

5.

STEP THREE

Directions: In your group, look over the list of suggestions in Step Two. Talk about the advantages and disadvantages of each of them. Try to decide which course of action you would take.

STEP FOUR

Directions: Complete the following sentences by putting a check mark in one of the three boxes. This step represents your personal opinion, so do it by yourself.

	Yes	*No*	*Not necessarily*
1. We should avoid any behavior that might bother our neighbors.	☐	☐	☐
2. People should have the right to live any way they want to as long as they don't cause direct harm to their neighbors.	☐	☐	☐
3. Living in an apartment usually requires us to accept and live with a certain amount of noise from our neighbors.	☐	☐	☐
4. It's easier for young people to complain face-to-face than it is for their parents.	☐	☐	☐
5. Landlords should be responsible for problems of human relations in their apartment buildings.	☐☐	☐☐	☐☐
6. Noisy tenants should be forced to move out.	☐☐	☐☐	☐☐

PIANO MURDERS STIR RESPONSE ... In October, the ... District Court sentenced a 47-year-old factory hand to death for killing a 33-year-old mother and her two daughters in ... in a fit of anger over piano noise from their apartment which constantly irritated him.

The ruling in the so-called piano murder case, which generally accepted the prosecution argument that an apartment occupant should bear noise to a certain extent, drew much criticism from those who considered themselves victims of noise pollution ...

The crime committed by the psychopath, who was found extremely sensitive to noise, raised the question of controlling noise in a crowded neighborhood and gave rise to groups of residents in opposition to such noise.

The murder case served at least to warn piano players to tone down out of regard for the feelings of their neighbors. ...

STEP FIVE

Directions: In your group, discuss your individual opinions about the ideas in Step Four.

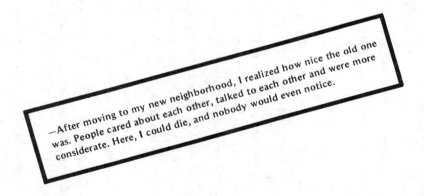

—After moving to my new neighborhood, I realized how nice the old one was. People cared about each other, talked to each other and were more considerate. Here, I could die, and nobody would even notice.

—After moving out of my old neighborhood, I felt like I had escaped from prison. There, everybody watched everybody else. You always had to worry about what the neighbors would say. Here I can come and go as I please. I hardly even know my neighbors.

Photo courtesy of The Gloucester Daily Times, Gloucester, Mass.

ADDITIONAL EXERCISES

1. Write an essay about either:
    (a) What you would do in a situation like this.
    (b) Any of the ideas in Step Four.
2. Write a dialog of or role play one of the following situations from the case study:
    (a) Your mother complains to the landlord about the noisy neighbor.
    (b) Your father talks to the old man about his grandson.
    (c) You talk to the noisy grandson yourself.
3. Read the newspaper article. Have you ever had any irritating problems with neighbors? What kind?
4. Read the quotes. What kind of neighborhood would you like to live in?
5. Write a short essay describing some person in your neighborhood.
6. Why do you think it is that in some countries people surround their houses with walls?
7. Read Robert Frost's poem, "Mending Wall." Discuss its meaning.

Getting

Involved

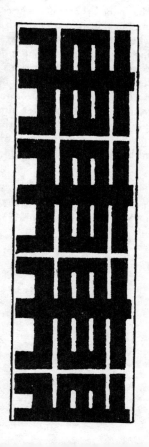

11

On one occasion a lawyer came forward to put this test question to him: 'Master, what must I do to inherit eternal life?' Jesus said, 'What is written in the Law? What is your reading of it?' He replied, 'Love the Lord your God with all your heart, with all your soul, with all your strength, and with all your mind; and your neighbour as yourself.' 'That is the right answer,' said Jesus; 'do that and you will live.'

But he wanted to vindicate himself, so he said to Jesus, 'And who is my neighbour?' Jesus replied, 'A man was on his way from Jerusalem down to Jericho when he fell in with robbers, who stripped him, beat him, and went off leaving him half dead. It so happened that a priest was going down by the same road; but when he saw him, he went past on the other side. So too a Levite came to the place, and when he saw him went past on the other side. But a Samaritan who was making the journey came upon him, and when he saw him was moved to pity. He went up and bandaged his wounds, bathing them with oil and wine. Then he lifted him on to his own beast, brought him to an inn, and looked after him there. Next day he produced two silver pieces and gave them to the innkeeper, and said, "Look after him; and if you spend any more, I will repay you on my way back." Which of these three do you think was neighbour to the man who fell into the hands of the robbers?' He answered, 'The one who showed him kindness.' Jesus said, 'Go and do as he did.'

Luke 10:25-37

STEP ONE

Directions: Read the following story carefully. As you read it, put yourself into the story and consider what you would do if you observed such an event.

The time of day is about 7:30 in the evening. You are on your way home and are presently on a subway train which is about full. At one of the stops, a young man in his early twenties gets on the subway and sits down next to a middle-aged woman reading a book. The man looks like he might have been drinking a little. After a few minutes, he reaches into his pocket for a cigarette and lights up. There are signs on the subway which prohibit smoking. People usually obey the signs, since it is both dangerous and inconsiderate not to. The woman turns to the man and very politely says, "Excuse me, sir, but you aren't supposed to smoke on the subway." The man ignores her, so she once again says, "Excuse me, sir, but people don't usually smoke on the subway." The man looks at the woman and says, "Why don't you mind your own business, lady?" The woman closes her

The Golden Rule
in ten of the World's Great Religions

CHRISTIANITY:

". . . All things whatsoever ye would that men should do to you, do ye even so to them . . ."

 CONFUCIANISM:

"Do not unto others what you would not they should do unto you."

 BUDDHISM :

"In five ways should a clansman minister to his friends and familiars—by generosity, courtesy and benevolence, by treating them as he treats himself, and by being as good as his word."

 HINDUISM:

"Do not to others, which if done to thee, would cause thee pain."

 ISLAM   :

"No one of you is a believer until he loves for his brother what he loves for himself."

 SIKHISM :

"As thou deemest thyself so deem others. Then shalt thou become a partner in heaven."

 JUDAISM :

"What is hurtful to yourself, do not to your fellow man."

JAINISM :

"In happiness and suffering, in joy and grief, we should regard all creatures as we regard our own self."

 **ZOROASTRIANISM:**

"That nature only is good when it shall not do unto another whatever is not good for its own self."

 TAOISM   :

"Regard your neighbor's gain as your own gain and regard your neighbor's loss as your own loss."

book, very calmly stands up, looks straight at the man and says, "I think the safety of all the passengers is everyone's business, young man." She then turns to walk away, when suddenly the young man jumps up and grabs her by the arm and turns her around. The woman yells.

What would you do at this point?

STEP TWO

Directions: Break up into groups. Read the possible courses of action below. As a group, add to this list other possible courses of action that you can think of. At this time do not try to evaluate the suggestions; just try to list as many as you can.

1. You can act like you don't see what is happening.
2. You can ask some of the other people on the train to help you restrain the man.
3. You can grab the man and push him down on the seat, so the woman can get away.
4.

5.

HANDBAG THIEF NABBED—Police arrested ———— a 32-year-old bathtub dealer of ———— near here, on a charge of snatching a handbag containing $———— from Mrs. ————, 53, of ———— at 11 a.m. Saturday.

———— was charged with robbery. According to his confession, he hit Mrs. ———— with a crowbar as she came out of the ———— Credit Association's head office and ran away.

Mrs. ———— cried for help, and three men, including a storekeeper, chased the robber for about 500 meters and overpowered him, police said.

GIVE ME A HAND Don't butt in where you're not wanted. A REAL LIFE-SAVER

Think of the others.

COOL IT MAN

mind your own business Bridge Over Troubled Waters

Lend me a hand

a helping hand I'm lookin' out for ol' number one.

The good Samaritan NOSY Do something!

DON'T PUSH! bug off

help me out

MY BROTHER'S KEEPER I'M SORRY.

Easy Man

If I want your help, I'll ask for it.

Don't bother me. It's none of my business.

STEP THREE

Directions: In your group, look over the list of suggestions in Step Two. Talk about the advantages and disadvantages of each of them. Try to decide which course of action you would take.

STEP FOUR

Directions: Complete the sentences on page 95 by putting a check mark in one of the three boxes. This step represents your personal opinion, so do it by yourself.

	Always do	Do in some cases	Never do
1. To help other people in trouble is something a person should . . .	□	□	□
2. To insist on what is right is something a person should . . .	□	□	□
3. To tell other people what is right or customary is something a person should . . .	□	□	□
4. To defend a principle is something a person should . . .	□	□	□
5. To mind your own business is something a person should . . .	□	□	□
6. To use force to defend yourself or another person is something a person should . . .	□	□	□

STEP FIVE

Directions: In your group, discuss your individual opinions about the ideas in Step Four.

ADDITIONAL EXERCISES

1. Write a dialog or role play a situation in which you see an older boy or girl of about fourteen hitting a small child of about eight. You go up to them and talk to the older boy/girl.
2. Suppose you saw a young man and woman arguing in public, but were too far away to hear what they were saying. If the man suddenly struck the woman, what would be your first thought or reaction? Are there any laws in your country against such an action?
3. Choose one alternative in the case study and write it up, describing what happens.
4. In some countries if a person hits another person who has not first hit him/her for any reason at all, regardless of whether he is in the right or wrong, he or she is fined or imprisoned. Do you think such a law is a good way to prevent violence in society? What are the laws in your country regarding one person hitting another person?
5. Look at the Golden Rule on p. 92. Do you think each means basically the same thing?
6. Look at the idioms on p. 94. What do you think they mean and in what situations would they be used?

A Friend in Need of Help

12

Photo courtesy of Royal Danish Ministry for Foreign Affairs, Copenhagen, Denmark

But of all plagues, good Heaven, thy wrath can send
Save, save, oh save me from the candid friend.

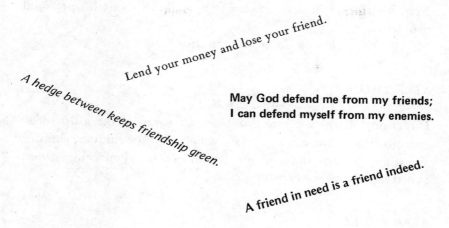

Lend your money and lose your friend.

A hedge between keeps friendship green.

**May God defend me from my friends;
I can defend myself from my enemies.**

A friend in need is a friend indeed.

STEP ONE

Directions: Read the following story carefully. As you read it, put yourself into the story and consider what you would do if you were Sol's friend.

You and Sol have been friends for over fifteen years. You went to high school together and now work in the same company. For the past several months, Sol has been very irritable and at times has shown his emotions by openly criticizing the company and some of his fellow workers. Most of the people in the office know that he sometimes drinks too much when he feels depressed about some of his personal and family problems.

But recently Sol made a very nasty personal comment which hurt one of the people in the office. No one said anything to him, but it was obvious that many people were angry at what he said and now have little sympathy for him.

You are beginning to wonder whether you should say something to Sol. You don't consider him your best friend, but you have been friends for a long time, and would hate to see him possibly lose his job because you didn't try to help him. On the other hand, you don't know whether Sol would think that you were interfering in his private life by talking about his personal problems.

What would you do in this situation?

STEP TWO

Directions: Break up into groups. As a group, make a list of all the possible courses of action which you could take in this situation. At this time do not try to evaluate your suggestions; just try to list as many as you can.

STEP THREE

Directions: Look over your list of suggestions. Talk about the advantages and disadvantages of each of them. Try to decide which course of action you would take.

> major rept issued by Natl Inst on Alcohol Abuse and Alcoholism finds alcoholism and related problems are costing nation more than $25-billion per yr, and that most Amer youths are occasional drinkers; lists econ consequences of alcohol abuse as lost work, med expenses and vehicle accidents, noting that in '71 estimated cost was $25.3-billion; inst dir Dr. Morris E. Chafetz says several recent studies reveal that occasional drinking by teen-agers is becoming nearly universal and that trend has increased sharply in last few yrs; notes surveys of hs students, which indicate 36% are drunk at least 4 times per yr and 1 in 7 males is drunk once per wk; says alcohol control laws and regulations are grossly ineffective in dealing with alcohol problems and often exacerbate them; rept cites evidence showing heavy drinking increases risk of cancer of mouth and throat; other findings discussed: 219-page document was prepared by 38-member task force under chmnship of Chafetz (L), Jl 11.1:1; comment (S), Jl 14.7:3
>
> —*New York Times Index,* 1974, Vol. A—M

STEP FOUR

Directions: Give your opinions about the sentences below by putting a check mark in one of the three boxes. This step represents your personal opinion, so do it by yourself.

	True	Not necessarily true	False
1. There is little a person can do to change the course of another person's life.	☐	☐	☐
2. You should not let personal matters interfere with a friendship.	☐	☐	☐
3. The course of your life is primarily beyond your own control.	☐	☐	☐
4. To try to help your friends improve their character is a good way to be a friend.	☐	☐	☐
5. People have to see with their own eyes in order to help improve themselves.	☐	☐	☐

STEP FIVE

Directions: In your group, discuss your individual opinions about the ideas in Step Four.

ADDITIONAL EXERCISES

1. Write an essay about either:
   (*a*) What you would do if you were in the situation in this case study.
   (*b*) Any of the ideas in Step Four.
2. Look at the sayings and quotes concerning friends. Discuss in your group what you think the meaning of each one is. Explain to the members in your group some of the sayings from your own language concerning friends or friendship.
3. Discuss in your group what your ideas of friendship are. What are the limits of friendship? Should we ask our friends for anything? Should we tell our friends our opinions about their problems even if they don't ask us? Give examples of what you think "good friends" and "bad friends" do.
4. Do you think it is possible to become friends—real friends—with a person from a different culture, or with a person who speaks a different native language? What do you think other people might say? What kind of problems might develop as a result?
5. Alcoholism is a problem in many countries. If you had a friend who was an alcoholic, would you try to help him/her? How?
6. Sometimes it is said that a woman never has a best friend. Do you think it is easier for two men to become friends than it is for two women?

Watching
Television

13

... Youth Admits Slashings

A 14-year-old junior high school boy from ... was arrested ... Thursday on a charge of injuring nine women and girls with a knife.

The boy admitted to most of the crimes, police said. His victims included two 8-year-old girls .... He said he had taken the girls into a room of the ... Junior High School, tied their limbs and inflicted cuts on them Dec. 7. Each girl required one month of treatment for their wounds, police said.

Police also stated that on other occasions, he admitted to slashing women and girls on the streets as he passed by them on a bicycle.

The boy confessed that he assaulted his victims *because he could not contain the urge to slash women after watching midnight television programs.* [italics added]

Summarization of New York Times article by Les Brown
A survey of attitudes toward television by a service organization
(lobbiers for major users of TV advertising) concludes that mothers
of children 2—20 overwhelmingly approve of and consider television
programs of benefit to their children . . . Certain consumer groups
are skeptical about the validity of the survey . . .

STEP ONE

Directions: Read the following story carefully.

Peter is worried about his son, Eddie. Eddie spends most of
his free time in front of the TV set.

Peter thinks children should get outside and play—both for
the physical exercise it provides and for the chance it gives them
to learn about getting along with other children. Peter remembers
when he was a child, and how he used to use his imagination to
create all sorts of fun games. He has also become more concerned
about his son's TV watching habits after reading several alarming
reports about violence in television programs and its harmful
effects on children.

He has made indirect remarks to his son, suggesting that it
might be more fun to go outside and play or to read an exciting
adventure story. But Eddie has not caught the hint, or, if he has,
he is ignoring it.

One evening Peter talks to his wife Carol. He thinks they
should make some rules to limit Eddie's TV watching. He

suggests that they should limit both the amount and the type of his TV viewing, since he would prefer to have his son watch some educational programs rather than just Westerns, cartoons and detective stories. Carol points out that he sets a bad example for his son by spending late evenings and many Sundays watching old movies or sports programs. Also, some of the sports programs, like boxing or wrestling, are very violent, Carol feels. Eddie regularly sees his father's TV viewing behavior. Carol thinks, therefore, that it would be unfair to impose rules on their son if her husband does not first of all modify his own habits. She says that would be hypocritical and would weaken their son's respect for them.

STEP TWO

Directions: Break up into groups. As a group, make a list of all the possible courses of action which Peter and Carol could take in this situation. At this time, do not try to evaluate your suggestions; just try to list as many as you can.

STEP THREE

Directions: Look over your list of suggestions. Talk about the advantages and disadvantages of each of them. Try to decide which course of action you think Peter and Carol should take.

STEP FOUR

Directions: Complete the sentences below by putting a check mark in one of the three boxes. This step represents your personal opinion, so do it by yourself.

	Very important	*Important*	*Not so important*
1. For children to spend a lot of time outdoors playing with other children is . . .	☐	☐	☐
2. For children to have a voice in deciding how they spend their own time is . . .	☐	☐	☐
3. For parents to practice what they preach is . . .	☐	☐	☐
4. For children to be protected or prevented from seeing violence on television is . . .	☐	☐	☐
5. For parents to limit what kind of TV programs their children can watch is . . .	☐	☐	☐

	Good	All right	Not good
6. For parents to tell their children how they should spend their time is . . .	☐	☐	☐
7. For children to spend a lot of time watching television is . . .	☐	☐	☐
8. For parents to spend a lot of time watching television is . . .	☐	☐	☐
9. For children to watch a lot of cartoons, Westerns, detective stories and monster programs is	☐	☐	☐

If you were born before, say, 1950, television came into your life after the formative years as just another medium. Even if you are now an "addict," it will be difficult for you to comprehend the transformations it has wrought. Could you, as a twelve-year-old, have contemplated spending an average of six hours *a day* at the local movie house? Not only would most parents not have permitted such behavior but most children would not have imagined the possibility. Yet, in our sample of children, nearly half the twelve-year-olds watch at least six hours of television every day.

George Gerbner and Larry Gross: Living with Television: The Violence Profile. The Annenberg School of Communications, *Journal of Communication,* 1976, Vol. 26, No. 2, p. 176.

STEP FIVE

Directions: In your group, discuss your individual opinions about the ideas in Step Four.

ADDITIONAL EXERCISES

1. Write a description of your favorite TV program when you were a child.
2. Why do you think some people spend so much time watching TV? Are there more interesting things to do? What kind of extra-curricular activities or recreational facilities are available in your country or community?
3. Do most of your friends watch TV? Do your schoolmates or fellow office workers spend much time talking about TV?
4. Write Eddie's opinion about his parents' decision to limit his viewing time.
5. There has been a lot written recently in newspapers about violence on TV and the influence that it has on children. Do you think some TV programs are too violent? Do you think this has any influence on children?

6. Look at the summary on p. 105. Why do you think so many mothers approve of their children watching TV? How do you feel about it?

7. Get a TV schedule from a newspaper or a TV guide. What types of programs are shown at different times during the day?

Working

Wife

14

Photo courtesy of Royal Danish Ministry of Foreign Affairs, Copenhagen, Denmark

Photo courtesy of French Embassy Press & Information Division, New York

STEP ONE

Directions: Read the following story carefully.

Marlene is married and has a set of twins four years old. She is a registered nurse but has not worked since her children were born. She is now thinking about going back to work at a local hospital which has a real need for nurses, but her husband is not in favor of the idea. He doesn't think that it is a good idea to have someone else take care of their children or to send them to a nursery school. He also doesn't like the idea of occasionally having to cook for himself and the two children when Marlene would be working at night or on the weekends.

Marlene understands her husband's feelings and the problems which would be created by her working. But she feels that it is important for her to go back to work before she forgets most

Photo courtesy of French Embassy Press & Information Division, New York

of the nursing she learned. She is aware of the fact that the children would prefer to have her take care of them, but she thinks that they are old enough to understand and adjust to the situation. She feels that having someone else take care of them occasionally certainly would not hurt them. Sending them to a nursery school, which she has been thinking of doing anyway, would give them a chance to learn how to get along with other children.

Marlene has tried to get her husband to understand that many women feel a need to do something else besides always taking care of the house. She has also pointed out that if anything happened to him, she would be responsible for taking care of the children as well as possibly him and herself.

He agrees with most of her ideas but still has some reservations about her working.

STEP TWO

Directions: Break up into groups. As a group make a list of all the possible courses of action which Marlene and her husband could take. Give the details of each one such as the different times she could work and the ways to solve the problem of what to do about the children. At this time, do not try to evaluate your suggestions; just try to list as many as you can.

STEP THREE

Directions: Look over your list of suggestions. Talk about the advantages and disadvantages of each of them. Try to decide which course of action you think Marlene should take.

There's more to life than just cooking,
   washing and cleaning up after the kids and the old man.

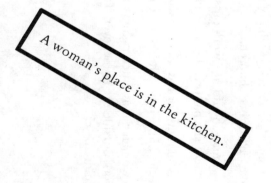

A woman's place is in the kitchen.

Kids need
full time mothers.

Woman-power: a country can't afford to waste it.

STEP FOUR

Directions: Give your opinions about the sentences below by putting a check mark in one of the three boxes. This step represents your personal opinion, so do it by yourself.

	Agree	*Disagree*	*Not necessarily*
1. A woman's main responsibility in life is to take care of her children.	☐	☐	☐
2. A woman should not work outside of the home if she has preschool age children.	☐	☐	☐
3. It is all right for a woman to work outside of the home if her children are in school.	☐	☐	☐
4. A woman has as much right as a man to work outside the home, even if she has children.	☐	☐	☐

□ □ □ □ □

□ □ □ □ □

□ □ □ □ □

5. A man should take equal responsibility with his wife for the housework and children, if his wife is working outside the home.

6. A woman should not work outside of the home if it means her husband has to cook or do housework occasionally.

7. It is important for a woman to have some kind of skill or profession in case of her husband's illness or death.

8. It is harmful for children if their mother is not home to take care of them.

9. It is a good experience for small children to go to a day care center or nursery school.

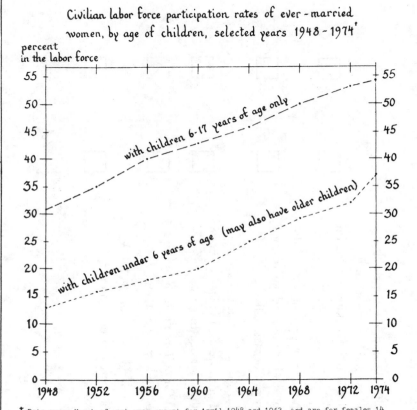

Mothers Are More Likely To Work Than Ever Before.
More Than Half of All Mothers of School Age
Children Were in the Labor Force in 1974.

Civilian labor force participation rates of ever-married
women, by age of children, selected years 1948-1974[†]

percent
in the labor force

with children 6-17 years of age only

with children under 6 years of age (may also have older children)

[†] Data cover March of each year except for April 1948 and 1952, and are for females 14 years of age and over except in 1968, 1972 and 1974, which are for 16 years and over.

Source: U.S. Department of Labor, Bureau of Labor Statistics.

STEP FIVE

Directions: In your group, discuss your individual opinions about the ideas in Step Four.

Photo courtesy of Royal Danish Ministry of Foreign Affairs, Copenhagen, Denmark

ADDITIONAL EXERCISES

1. Write what you think the twins' opinion would be about their mother going to work.
2. Write an essay describing how and by whom you were taken care of when you were small.
3. Do you or did you ever have to help take care of your brothers and sisters? If so, why? What did you do?
4. Write a dialog between Marlene and a single working friend.
5. Do you think a mother's love is any different or more important than the love given to a child by a professional nurse, nursery attendant, brother or sister, neighbor, grandparent, or some other person taking care of the child? If you think there is a big difference, why?

6.　Look at the chart on p. 120. Explain what the chart means. Do you think the statistics on working women in your country are similar?

7.　Look at the sayings on p. 117. What do they mean? Are there any similar expressions in your country?

Your Friend's a Thief

AN EYE FOR AN EYE

HONESTY'S THE BEST POLICY

You reap what you sow

GOOD GUYS FINISH LAST

CHARITY STARTS AT HOME

If you live by the rules, you'll never get ahead

It's every guy for himself

It's a dog eat dog world

One thrill isn't worth a lifetime of misery

Shoplifting, once considered a
minor problem mostly involving
juveniles and kleptomaniacs, has
become one of the country's
fastest-growing crimes and is
costing merchants $5-billion a
year.

Excerpt from *The New York Times,* Dec. 24, 1974.

STEP ONE

Directions: Read the following story carefully. As you read it,
put yourself into the story and imagine what you would do if
you were faced with such a problem.

You have been working as a sales clerk in a men's
department store for two years and feel quite satisfied with your
job. The store is a new one that is steadily growing. You think
that the chances are pretty good that you can eventually be
promoted to a more responsible and well paying position.

A couple of days ago, though, something happened that put
you in a difficult position. You discovered that another clerk in
your department was stealing goods from the store.

Your supervisor had told you several weeks before that
some goods were missing and asked you to keep an eye out for
shoplifting by customers or stealing by employees. If you expose
the thief, your supervisor will realize your reliability as an
employee, and it might help your own career. Your future in the

company looks good and you don't want to risk it by protecting or covering up for the thief.

But you don't know exactly what to do since the clerk you caught is an old friend of yours from high school. About six months ago you introduced him to the personnel manager, and he was hired. At that time you were glad he got the job since he had said that he really needed the money because of some medical expenses in his family. When you caught him stealing he asked you not to tell the store since losing the job would increase the burden on his family. Besides, since the department store is a successful business, he doesn't think it will be hurt by the amount of goods he has taken. He has asked you, as a friend, to try to understand his situation and not say anything.

What do you think you should do?

STEP TWO

Directions: Break up into groups. As a group, make a list of all the possible courses of action which you could take. At this time, do not try to evaluate your suggestions; just try to list as many as you can.

STEP THREE

Directions: Look over your list of suggestions. Talk about the advantages and disadvantages of each one. Try to decide which course of action you would take in this situation.

STEP FOUR

Directions: Give your opinions about the sentences on the next page by putting a check mark in one of the three boxes. This step represents your personal opinion, so do it by yourself.

	Agree	Disagree	Not necessarily
1. Being loyal to friends is very important.	☐	☐	☐
2. Being loyal to your business or company is very important.	☐	☐	☐
3. Being a good friend sometimes requires us to risk our own job, family or reputation for the sake of our friends.	☐	☐	☐
4. Stealing is very wrong, and anyone who steals should be punished.	☐	☐	☐
5. If you work for a store or business, the financial success of that store is very important in your own life.	☐	☐	☐
6. The law is sometimes unjust since it does not consider human circumstances.	☐	☐	☐
7. Laws should be obeyed and should not be broken for personal reasons.	☐	☐	☐
8. Every person has a responsibility not only to obey the law, but also to expose other people who break it.	☐	☐	☐
9. Cases in which a law has been broken should be judged according to the relative circumstances rather than strictly by the law.	☐	☐	☐

Photo by Ed Wolkin courtesy of The Gloucester Daily Times, *Gloucester, Mass.*

STEP FIVE

Directions: In your group, discuss your individual opinions about the ideas in Step Four.

ADDITIONAL EXERCISES

1. Put yourself into the situation in the case study. Write a dialog between you and your friend whom you caught stealing.

2. Look at the excerpt on shoplifting in the U.S. (p. 125). Why do you think some people feel that there is nothing wrong with stealing or shoplifting?

3. What happens to people in your country who are caught stealing? In some countries thieves' fingers or hand are cut off as punishment. What do you think of this? How do you think thieves should be dealt with?

4. If someone in your school or office were stealing money from you and the other people, what would you do to try to catch him? When the person was caught what would you do to him?

5. Do you think Robin Hood's philosophy of stealing from the rich to give to the poor is justified?

6. In the U.S. high school and college students often steal traffic signs, beer mugs, ashtrays, etc., and put them in their rooms. Why do you think they do this? Is this done in your country? Have you ever stolen something similar?

7. Read the sayings on p. 124. What do they mean? What expressions do you have in your country about honesty, stealing, etc.?

Credits and Permissions

The authors and the publisher extend their thanks to the people and source organizations cited on text pages for permission to use the photographs in this book. As well, we are grateful to the following:

The quotation on page 7 is reprinted with the permission of *Encyclopaedia Britannica,* Inc., Chicago, Illinois.

The article on page 8, which appeared in 1975 in *The Asahi Evening News,* Tokyo, is reprinted with the permission of Ann Landers, Field Newspaper Syndicate.

The quotes on pages 12, 13, and 17 are reprinted with the permission of The Research Club in Language Learning.

The graph and quotation on page 33 are reprinted with the permission of Bob Weiss Associates for *Fortune* magazine.

The article on page 42 is reprinted from *Facts on File,* Vol. 35, No. 1798, pp. 278-279, April 26, 1975 with the permission of Facts on File, Inc.

The articles on pages 66 and 100 are reprinted with the permission of The New York Times Company.

The articles on pages 74, 86, 93, and 104 are reprinted with the permission of *The Japan Times,* Tokyo.

The Golden Rule on page 92 is reprinted with the permission of the Fellowship for Spiritual Understanding, Palos Verdes Estates, California.

The collage on page 107, comprised from parts of *TV Guide,* is reprinted with the permission of *TV Guide* magazine. Copyright © 1976 by Triangle Publications, Inc., Radnor, Pennsylvania.

The article on page 110 is reprinted with the permission of the Annenberg School of Communications, Philadelphia, Pennsylvania.

The chart on page 120 is reprinted with the permission of the Women's Bureau, U.S. Department of Labor.

Cartoons on pages 12, 48, and 106 are by John Redmond and those on pages 40, 57, 66, 67, and 82 are by Shigeru Usui.